FROM PARTNERS TO PARENTS

FROM PARTNERS TO PARENTS

Transitioning to Parenthood Together

AVERY NIGHTINGALE

Creative Quill Press

CONTENTS

CHAPTER 1

Introduction

The transition to parenthood is a unique and significant time in a person's life. While research on the topic of becoming a parent (especially for the first time) abounds, a great deal of the focus centers on the experiences and outcomes of the mother. This is likely due to the range of significant physical and hormonal changes that childbirth and lactation uniquely bring, along with the fact that many studies still only include women. Despite these study focuses, the birth or adoption of a child is the most common way in which men also become parents. Inspired by gender transformation theory, we draw attention to the concept of partnership: relationships which have been categorized as being especially equitable and intimate, or companionate. As with unmarried couples, trans men having children, and others, same-sex couples' transitions to parenthood are also understudied. In short, the motivation for this book was inspired by both robust support in the popular media that having children changes relationships and the need to measure these changes through diverse types of families.

The goal of this edited volume was to extend the understanding of the transition to parenthood to a broad view that centers around the needs of currently parented and intending families. Specifically, this book is focused on parents who are sharing the experience of transitioning to parenthood, considered together as a unit. Life transitions can make or break a relationship. They bind with some relationships and separate, or shift the dynamics of, others. We also focus on the theme of family equality – the ability for the couple to divide labor and finances fairly – through discussions of timecourse divisions, feminism, and social equality theories. Throughout the book, the importance of studying the experiences of diverse parents becoming parents is highlighted. This book is intended to help researchers and practitioners broaden and deepen knowledge and resources for these transitions so that they may develop policies and services that assist all types of families as they begin or expand their families.

CHAPTER 2

Understanding Parenthood

It may be that our views of parenthood can shift most dramatically when we face heading into parenthood ourselves. Because we are not authority figures or employers, because we no longer see children in strictly mechanistic terms (as with child brides), our transformation in perspective in anticipatory - as we begin or consider beginning parenthood, a process Kitty Chisholm called "ante-natal" personhood. We become active agents who are partners in our shared parenthood for some indeterminable period of time, rather than individuals who will simply become parents one day, as we learn how to do that in tandem (or not) with partners who are themselves entering or avoiding parenthood, all while distinguishing this from some presumed autonomy or individual process, given that what happens between us seems to inform what will happen. This period, as Chisholm describes in her study, is also when we can choose to parent independently rather than (or concurrently with) relying on other co-parents or legal and commercial societies.

Once couples become pregnant, many are confronted with their automatic assumptions about motherhood, like that women are more nurturing and better caretakers for children. People mean well, of course, as they give us lessons in gender essentialism. Some expectant parents find themselves questioning both these assumptions and their friendships with people who hold them. The situation is often made worse for LGBT couples who are frequently asked who the real mom or real dad is. People, unaware of what they imply about non-biological parents given that it's impossible for two women and two men to be biological parents together, don't recognize their complicity in imposing particular maternal and paternal roles on us and our future children. And even though it is right if more people see gay and lesbian relationships as loving and just as capable of raising children as everyone else, the devaluation of non-biological parenthood, including its invisibility in popular portrayals of parent-child relationships, is largely untouched.

CHAPTER 3

Preparing for Parenthood

Couples also need to consider the ways the baby impacts their physical, emotional, sexual, and identity life. Wives expect and report higher degrees of emotional support compared to their husbands. Experience with emotional regulation is what differentiates both genders. Reassuringly, happy parents have a happy baby. When babies get discharged home from the hospital, often both parents feel equally competent caring for their infant. Nevertheless, principal caregivers tend to be firmer with their babies in choosing play objects that are safer. We also know that men respond more quickly than women when their babies start crying. It seems the traditional division of domestic roles promoted gender-specific parenting styles respectively, with men perceived to be the strict disciplinarian. The secure attachment of the baby to the mom partly depends on whether the father is in the picture. In homes where the father is the principal caregiver, relationships are further enhanced and bonded by skin-to-skin bonding. Importantly, dads are likely to better understand and respond to their own babies. This seems similar to the premise of the ABCD Mobile Therapy where familiar landmarks create avenues for easier understanding and interactions.

Many couples do not discuss their expectations surrounding parenting before the baby comes. Many expectant parents have similar romanticized expectations about how parenthood will look and feel. The challenge many may not have anticipated is dealing with an unexpected, crying, colicky baby, and the emotional and physical life, relationship, financial, and identity issues. Having realistic expectations and discussing conflict resolution strategies, parenting roles and needs, finances, and family planning makes becoming parents for the very first time lessen the blow.

CHAPTER 4

Nurturing Your Relationship

One of the dangers of a marriage or partnership is varying expectations about how much time and attention a child should receive. One of the interview respondents encapsulated some common sentiments about being a new parent: Though it's tempting to dedicate all of yourself to your baby, the two of you need a break every once in a while. Selecting some time for your relationship is an incredibly valuable investment in your future together. Often in first-time parenting situations, one partner feels less interested in (or able to handle) spending time away from the child. This person is usually the mother, which only makes a new parent getaway more critical: it gives the mom a break from the baby and helps her maintain her sense of self to some extent by giving her a rare opportunity to spend time away in the time-consuming presence of her partner. Being a parent should never stop you from being a couple, because doing so will only result in implosion of the partnership.

Though caring for your baby and managing the changes in your life are sure to consume much of your time, nurturing your relationship with your partner is just as - if not more - important than ever. Ideally, you and your partner will become closer through the birth of your child, as a direct result of raising a child together. But in order for you to benefit from that raised sense of intimacy, you need to invest in nurturing your relationship. Both time and effort oriented in the direction of your partner are necessary to maintaining - not to mention strengthening - the love between you and combating the stress that overburdened new parents often experience.

CHAPTER 5

Communicating Effectively

Effective communication through honesty and openness creates an environment where you can pour out the flood of concerns swirling around in your head. Your partner can pour out his or her thoughts and plans too. It can be tempting to focus solely on immediate needs and wants instead of really addressing the deeply rooted issues. When both of you are mulling over things on your own and not expressing any opinions (both partners) or expressing only surface-level commitment (one partner), it leaves unknowns to be surface at the least convenient times: while labor is pressing, or when Unit Baby sleeps in 40-minute intervals. Not communicating or only sharing part of your thoughts as a parent will make times of high stress terrible. Part of a transition to parenthood is developing effective ways of communicating with your partner so the two of you can tackle these vaguely spoken topics. There are specific strategies that work really well. Recognizing, acknowledging, and respecting the honest basis of effective communication as we talk through some additional aspects of making a dialogue with your partner helpful will give you building blocks toward real progress.

Talking to your partner honestly and respectfully is the heart of good communication. Throughout this book, we have stressed the importance of open and honest communication. We really do believe that all other good things flow from really understanding each other. Pregnancy is a time when you're going to hear each other's feelings and thoughts about parenting much more than usual. It fosters a desire to create a parenting plan together. Approaching your discussions with respect for each other's point of view creates a solid relationship foundation for co-parenting and opens the door to really connecting in deep and meaningful ways. Effective management of the increased conversational opportunities will save time, reduce unnecessary sources of worry, foster growth, and build trust that will serve you well throughout your journey as parents. Just like with a GPS, the effective input of both partners will go a long way toward minimizing the many little detours (and fast-food runs) that could have on a whim you take on this parenting journey.

CHAPTER 6

Managing Expectations

One recent large-scale study of new parents at Cornell University found that the length of a couple's relationship was related to how closely their perceptions matched each other and that these discrepancies were associated with concurrent feelings of dissatisfaction. The further the partners were from each other in terms of their perceived agreement on expectations for household and childcare responsibilities and their division of tasks, the more dissatisfied they were with their relationship. Furthermore, we found that communication quality in general, as well as how individuals addressed unmet expectations, was associated with adjustment for both men and women. While most parents we have surveyed saw multiple marital and co-parenting aspects as falling short of their pre-birth expectations, those who responded to these unmet expectations by seeking change through negotiation or seeking support from spouses or friends tended to adjust better to parenthood.

Too often, unmet expectations lead to disappointment, frustration, and anger and can become a major source of conflict. During the nesting phase, managing each other's expectations is key. What we learned through our clinic's work and from our new research is that it is not the fact that individuals have unrealistic expectations that is the problem. It is, rather, the fact that partner perceptions of each other's expectations are often so widely discrepant. In other words, you may think you know what your partner expects only to find out that you are rather clueless.

CHAPTER 7

Balancing Responsibilities

In this context, participants in the present study alluded to different roles which they perceived as more beneficial to be taken on. Despite the potential differences, they rated themselves as equally sharing caregiving responsibilities and they were proud about their fathering identity. Women no longer can dominate as tasks such as household chores were perceived to have equalled out between couples, with many magic happening unseen and in unknown places. Having children altered their interaction with time and the environment and consequently, each actor would have to do his or her best to influence or respond effectively to the altered system otherwise unnoticed.

We felt like the chaos was becoming more routine as we were finding ways to cope with it in a new way. It is becoming more familiar and manageable, and less quantifiable as time passes. We are finding ways to work with it, around it, or through it – within articulated maturities in how we relate to each other or to the external world. In hindsight, that's the best thing about being "us" to this day. The idea of balance of obligations or responsibilities was also conspicuously noted among most of the individuals. Given the couples' employment and commitments beyond parenting, the balance of both responsibilities emerged as a recurring theme in the interviews. Couples openly noted that certain responsibilities were being fulfilled well by either one of them, such as caregiving and financial support (they have depended financially on the other person for two years following the birth of the child).

CHAPTER 8

Creating a Supportive Environment

The support of the couple toward each other in the process of parenting is not limited to a set of tasks, but to having their family functional and committed to helping each other with a spirit of unity. When parents focus on each other, children benefit from feeling safe, secure, and stable. On the other hand, when the focus is on the children, the contribution of the couple runs the risk of breaking up, making them become two isolated people living under the same roof. Therefore, it is essential that there be good communication that will allow the couple to function as one in a spirit of unity.

Go easy on the other, because they are both changing and learning in this new phase. And always compliment good actions and recognize the strength of one another. As partners, it is essential to encourage the other, as this has been greatly noticed during the studies. Communication is a fundamental pillar for any relationship, however maintaining a family, especially after the arrival of a child, requires that there be a strong fabric to add to the communication between the couple. Learning to communicate becomes an imperative need, both to improve what is already correct and to heal what is wrong. It is necessary to ensure a healthy and non-stressful environment where everyone actively participates in raising their children.

Here are my tips for communicating more effectively in a new family and how to create a supportive environment to be able to better connect with your partner, creating a more harmonious relationship. As a couple and even before the baby arrives, it is essential to create a supportive climate in the relationship to strengthen the couple, especially during the big change that is happening. Learn to listen and temper your reactions before jumping without even analyzing the situation is important. Identify from the outside what is most important at the moment of crisis and recognize the importance of the other for both your life and your baby.

CHAPTER 9

Embracing Changes

We all need to accept the notion that no matter how much we may want them to remain small, our children will grow up to become independent, autonomous individuals. As undesirable as we might find it, intact relationships with greatest frequency are the result of one partner lovingly accepting the concept, "he is who he is, and I shall not attempt to mold him to something different." The need for unconditional acceptance extends not only to our children but also to their parents. In light of the challenges of having and rearing kids, our romantic relationships the aspect of allowing friends and colleagues to witness our lives as a family unit becomes even more important. It is through regular interactions with those outside of the family that we may be more likely to take our co-parenting role seriously. Being 'good parents' is much more than meeting the physical, emotional, and spiritual needs of children. Lean on one another for support and kindness during difficult times. And through being good and supportive partners, you may indeed become the very best parents.

The sleepless nights and emotionally charged days of early parenthood can strain even the most committed partners. But don't despair. One of the most distinct and cherished elements of a romantic relationship that becomes a family relationship is shared laughter. You won't remember with fondness how tired you were getting up at 3:00 a.m. to diaper, swaddle, and feed your newborn. Instead, you will remember and laugh about the time one or both of you forgot to replace the stroller back in the car after unloading it and then, while struggling to manage to make it through Target, suddenly realized that it was back in the parking lot, which was 1/2 mile away.

CHAPTER 10

Coping with Stress

We did not find a lot of instances where partners were directly helping each other during stressful events, but we believe that emotional support plays a more prominent role during other times in parenthood. There were a few instances (of a total 536) when the partner demonstrated mastery of a situation and sought delegated help, but these constituted only 3.9% of the total. In almost 31% of the couples' interactions, both partners were unsuccessful. The couple rarely argued with each other. When it happened (3.6% of the time), disapproval was not expressed in front of the child during stressful events; 3.2% of the time there were aggressive glances, which the authors did not count as an argument.

We have observed some ways that new parents cope with stress. One approach is strategic thinking, whereby partners construe the situation as challenging but then rationalize possible benefits. They may find comfort that their difficulties are temporary and that others are worse off than they are. By rehearsing positive attributes of their child and focusing on the future, new parents can deflect attention from frustration and stay engaged in their caregiving role. When dealing with their own internal upset, partners encourage each other with gentle affirmations or fiery pep talks. Whether receiving encouragement from a partner or reminding their partner of potential growth opportunities and reasons for optimism, our findings suggest that parents may use positive interpersonal processes to regulate their emotions in ways that benefit themselves and their children.

CHAPTER 11

Maintaining Self-Care

Developing self-care is important because it can alter negative effects on the relationship as well (which is part of the dyad commands to the development and maintenance of stress, well-being, and couple's care reciprocity, as well as in interactions and relational satisfaction). These commands state how the dyad can affect relationship quality, while relational satisfaction plays a role in regard to self-perceived personal belongingness, and one's inclusivity within relationship assessments. It is emphasized that happy and satisfied individuals gain aesthetic rewards by way of their significant others, which allows forming satisfying bonds in one's lifetime where self-transformation determines one's inner qualities in founding faithful and successful romantic relationships.

Lastly, maintaining one's self-care is important in order to maintain a state of homeostasis. This includes self-assertion, which is speaking up for one's needs and rights by taking time for oneself. Self-care also allows individuals to communicate to partners that by taking care of oneself, one can also take care of themselves in the best way. This advice encourages individuals to repeatedly assess their partner relationships, while if all 3 aspects of the relationship (self, partner, and child) are negatively affected, therapy would be beneficial. Assertive self-confidence enables recognition, acceptance, and encouragement to balance demands, resist peer pressure, seek family support, and value productive time. Indeed, by adopting statements pointed out in the emotional responses within a relationship (such as: "I should take care of myself, keep my mood and behavior in moderation; I should balance personal and couple's time with time to a family member or other person; I have to set boundaries"). By doing so, one is less likely to feel a negative effect of the transition to parenthood.

CHAPTER 12

Parenting Styles and Strategies

The parents' own childhood experiences, personal beliefs, and values generally determine their dominant style of handling the challenges of the new parent role. They then adapt their style a little to meet the individual needs and feedback of their child. The exercise of authority has been tending to reconfigure over the years and the current coexistence of three generations in the workplace is likely to influence these changes. It is possible to notice that traditional forms of authority seem to be in the process of changing, suggesting that the current younger generations seek to trust the influence of authority by opting for a softer, more flexible and participative parenting style, the objective of which is to stimulate understanding, respect, and self-control. These characteristics were predominantly associated with higher levels of education and higher levels of resources.

In the framework of balancing dual-career households with parenthood, most of the research on parenting styles suggests advantages in the authoritative style, promoting positive attitudes and behavior in children, as well as being beneficial for the parents in terms of how satisfied they are with their roles and their quality of life as a couple. Where the parent focuses more on caregiving and less on decision-making (often resulting from problems of work and family conciliation), the relationship of the couple with the child may appear to be colder, even if the child's biopsychosocial development does not seem to be endangered.

Finding a suitable parenting style or creating a balance that works for both parents or caregivers is critical in the successful transition to parenthood, as well as laying the foundation for healthy child development. In recent years, research has focused on two dimensions involved in this decision-making process: authoritative and involved parenting. The first dimension places high on levels of responsiveness and demandingness, while the second is characterized by high levels of involvement.

CHAPTER 13

Bonding with Your Baby

Even when nothing is technically wrong, taking care of a baby can still be filled with difficult moments and challenges. In normal, healthy human development, there is built-in risk. Your baby is not yet tough enough to master their emotions like you are, and your new baby's demands have no rhythm and do not follow human schedules. How do babies tell us what they want? They do not talk and they do not have scheduled amazing things like when they need burping, a dirty diaper, or something else. Child-rearing is, beyond any shadow of a doubt, a baby-whispering job; it is very time-consuming and complicated. Your baby communicates with you through their behavior, which is determined by their feelings. It is you who must make sense of your baby's needs, and this understanding will come to fruition. In child-rearing and baby-whispering, you will become a true expert!

Even after we've become parents, we need to first focus on our relationships, namely with our partners, before we can bond with our baby. This is called a couple-centered approach to help your baby. Let the two of you deal with how you work together and how to adjust your lives together, as well as dealing with your feelings and behaviors so you can get close to your new baby. Remember, the parenting of any child is an evolutionary process; it involves stability, volatility, and the creation of family routines. In this chapter, we strive to detail behaviors, feelings, and attitudes that are required to facilitate this evolutionary process. First, we introduced the general principles that guide our thinking. Next, we explained the need for a parental approach to focus more on your couple relationship because this is essentially important at the start of being a first-time parent. Then, we talked about behaviors that are needed by each one of you, who is your baby's first caregiver. This includes handling the baby, so you will gain confidence.

CHAPTER 14

Sharing Parenting Duties

Mothers who "gatekeep," or control the way and amount of a father's involvement with the couple's child or children, have been found to discourage greater father involvement. To encourage involved fathering in your partnership, decrease "gatekeeping" behaviors and communicate openly about your hopes and concerns. As fathers have greater caregiving responsibilities, they need positive reinforcement from partners and others, as well as permission to overcome their insecurities or fears about inadequate parenting.

By contrast, fathers who are actively involved in caring for their children report higher life satisfaction and lower rates of depression, and partner support is an essential predictor of quality caregiving by fathers. Involved fathers are also linked to a variety of positive child outcomes, including improved cognitive development and higher socioemotional maturity, as well as a lower risk for early behavior problems.

A recent survey analyzed data collected over six decades from 30,000 men and women and observed that couples who equally shared in the caregiving had the highest overall levels of marital quality. In contrast, for more traditional couples, the more a woman became pregnant and gave birth, the more likely she was to report decreased satisfaction with the marriage.

Feeling good about the division of parenting labor in your home contributes significantly to your overall satisfaction with your relationship. Moreover, nailing the division of labor caregiving has positive implications for the well-being of each partner, for the strength of your partnership—really!—and for your child.

CHAPTER 15

Building a Strong Parenting Team

However, soon after the arrival of the baby, a parenthood bubble forms around the young mother, depriving the father of his usual privileges. In doing so, moms strive to limit the sources of family stress. This dynamic, which begins with the best intentions, often leads to a distancing of the new father from the mother and the newborn, as well as from his family environment. In reality, this protective withdrawal of the mother is harmful to the couple's relationship, since it can lead to feelings of exclusion in the father and underlie conflict in the co-parenting relationship. In the face of this void left in the family and in their fathering role, the father can reduce his investment in the conjugal relationship and consequently fail to maintain it. It thus loses its sense of place in a relationship with no apparent benefits for him. He may then develop feelings of shame for his inability to control the crucial aspects of his life, namely his relationships with his loved ones.

One of the strongest predictors of happiness for mothers of infants is the quality of their relationship with their partner. Therefore, it is not surprising that satisfied couples' relationships also play a significant role in the quality of their parenting relationship. But relationships engineers that are couples must adapt to parenthood and to evolving needs, being facing a unique set of challenges. Strengthening the intimate relationship has an obvious benefit for all couples except that children grow up in an environment where they experience an increasing sense of security, as well as favorable relational models. Research seems to reveal that, more than the individual characteristics of the parents, it is the quality of the couple's relationship that determines the harmonious development of their children.

CHAPTER 16

Establishing Routines and Boundaries

Initially, it may not be easy to establish routines. Without negotiating an obvious and accepted plan of action, things did not go well in the beginning. There was no blueprint that told the couple what to do when Jane was born and Edward and Margaret were new parents. Everything was up for grabs and took some negotiation. They soon realized that it was unfair for Margaret to do all the nighttime feedings for the new baby, simply because she was home during the day. They also decided that it was not healthy for Edward to be the only person going to work in his family to earn an income. Edward agreed to split the nighttime feedings with his wife. This change in routine was possible, although understandably, two people were affected. For example, Edward was tired during the weekends when Margaret gave him the opportunity to nap after the birth of their child. He sometimes chose not to nap, calling the moments "Father-Daughter time."

Get into the habit of establishing routines and boundaries in your relationship every day. Do not let problems fester. Constructive problem solving is crucial in marriage. Establishing routines and boundaries in your relationship from the very beginning certainly helped Margaret and Edward. When Margaret got up during the night with Jane, Edward would slip into a deep sleep. In the morning, Margaret usually carried the first load of baby clothes with her to the laundry room before Edward was fully awake. Sometimes he helped, but too often she did such things without thinking or communicating with him, expecting him to read her mind and realize all that she had done. On the other hand, when Margaret managed to get the baby to sleep and Edward woke Jane with over-tolerant baby talk, Margaret usually awakened the baby with a piercing glance.

CHAPTER 17

Promoting Child Development

Parental beliefs about society's expectations about the division of labor at home are also important to child development, particularly where expectations are not met. In their erroneous cross-sectional investigation, McClelland and colleagues found both mother and father beliefs about fathers' close involvement in their child's education to be important to their children's vocabulary skills, beliefs that were more important than the parent's actual close involvement in children's language development activities. Surprisingly, beliefs about fathers' involvement from fathers' predictive for their child's vocabulary skills than the close involvement fathers then actually has with their children. Rather, the stronger predictor of children's vocabulary skills was the belief of new fathers that fathers should be involved with their young children in their educational activities like telling stories and discussing educational media.

Parents' beliefs about child development and child rearing, as well as their own mental health, self-esteem, and self-efficacy, have been proven to be important determinants of sensitive and responsive caregiving practices. Doubts and disagreements about a partner's child care practices may contribute to one's self-doubt, anxiety, uncertainty, and concern about self and relationship competence. Feeling and being competent in caregiving, in contrast, can be a boost to parents' self-esteem, self-efficacy, and mental health that can contribute to more effective parenting. Unresolved individual doubts, mismatches, and disagreements about how to support child development can therefore intersect to threaten the stability and functioning of the whole family system by producing instability and fragmentation. This suggests that what people know or think about child development and the conditions established to support or hinder successful self and relationship development over the become very important during the transition to parenthood.

CHAPTER 18

Handling Sleep Challenges

If your child has had trouble sleeping through the night, don't worry too much. In terms of development, it is completely normal for babies who are breastfed (only) to wake up to eat in the nighttime until the age of 7 months, and it is not abnormal for many infants to need nourishment one or more times in the night after that. This is not a failure on the part of parents, but instead a result of babies' tiny stomachs and fast metabolism. If your child (no matter the age of the child) wakes and struggles with some aspect of sleep, remember that it may not be 100% about the babe needing something to eat, but manifesting even, could reflect some developmental gains being made, for example, motor skills (a baby has learned to crawl and now practices this skill in the bed; baby sat for the first time without losing balance and the absence of stability makes it difficult for the child to relax during his nap, etc.). For when your baby experiences a sleep regression, you will find helpful suggestions in section 13, "Sleep Regressions in Your Baby".

Establish a message in your relationship that "we can handle sleep challenges!" Mental rehearsal. Parents-to-be tend to spend a lot more time discussing the positives rather than the challenges of having a baby. Make sure to chat about some potential baby worries and how the two of you would want to handle them: "what if the baby has colic?...what if the baby doesn't sleep well?" Being well-adjusted to realistically expect some sleep issues and tackle them thoughtfully can help with expectations and mean fewer negative surprises and more positive, innovative strategies when they show up.

CHAPTER 19

Dealing with Discipline

Meet Wy and Willia. Willia is from Indonesia where people usually live with their extended families. However, Wy, the husband, is from America where the idea of a nuclear family is popular. Being a mother type who is caring and very supportive, Willia tends to be more permissive and lax when it comes to discipline. In contrast, Wy is firmer and tougher. He sets rules and enforces discipline. Typically, the roles of men and women in Indonesian culture emphasize that women are more nurturing and gentle, in contrast to men as more stern and strict in terms of matters regarding discipline, as well as the education of children is also formerly associated with women's duties. When men are made to be decision-makers in a family, they are more dominant in order to look responsible and protective of the family and, in the context of the above, shaping the personality and characteristics of a child is also considered a significant matter, which eventually reinforces parenting attitudes and discipline used on the children.

Yoon: The concern that I have is that the mother-in-law will give her a lot of candy and she will eat candy all the time, everywhere, and anytime, and she will become fat and unhealthy. That really worries me about how the mother-in-law will be like my mother and have rules against it, and have strong discipline against all the condiments.

From Partners to Parents: Transitioning to Parenthood Together. Caron: When it comes to discipline, we are quite different because Henry comes from a family of seven children and his family is traditional. But for me, I grew up with my grandparents alone and my parents were like friends.

CHAPTER 20

Encouraging Healthy Habits

Pregnancy produces unique opportunities for each partner to practice behaviors that support the other in their quest for good health. To put this section in context, one birth coach advised a man, "Treat her like a queen. Because one day she'll be treating you like a king." This philosophy is especially important during the childbearing year. Either or both partners in your couple might have already struggled with making exercise an important priority in their lives. Women at the end of the first trimester of pregnancy should get at least thirty minutes a day of moderate exercise on most, if not all, days. In addition to cardio like brisk walking, yoga, which "teaches us to ground ourselves into the moment, focus and concentrate," can help prevent falls by improving balance. For the average male, moderate aerobic exercise means working out for thirty minutes. Men should aim for aerobic exercise plus weight lifting on at least three days per week. Even better, for women, exercising during pregnancy is a huge support to the cardiovascular health of her man. In other words, when a man's activities support his partner's exercise, his heart-healthy activities support her heart.

Good nutrition, regular exercise, and adequate rest are important at any time in life. During the transition to parenthood, sticking to healthy habits can be challenging. The good news is, how a couple takes care of themselves after they have a baby matters little compared to how much they supported each other in healthy living during the pregnancy. Therefore, partners who encourage each other to practice healthy habits before birth also contribute to the likelihood that they will each be successful in maintaining good health habits after the baby is born. While the specifics about these healthy habits are well known, the message that a changing family needs to internalize is that each person's actions support the other's healthy habits and contribute to both people's sexual satisfaction, their relationship satisfaction, and their personal health.

CHAPTER 21

Navigating Parenting Challenges

Negative changes are frequently seen in other aspects of the relationship with the arrival of a child as well. In the transition to parenthood, the balance of power changes between couples. This shift often leads to tension. If a couple is not properly aware of the coming shift in power balance, they may interpret an otherwise normal competition between parenting styles as one partner trying to dominate the other. By understanding this dynamic as part of a larger system, a couple may be less prone to negative interpretations, and may interpret the challenges of being on a team as normal. In most health situations, team dynamics would be considered not only beneficial, but necessary. Unfortunately, couples often dismiss this idea.

Once the transition to parenthood is in full swing, couples have a myriad of new tasks to attend to, and these can be quite consuming. At this point, happy couples often lose their focus on each other and their own relationship. They become more absorbed in the practical parts of life. Even though they talk to each other about baby-related activities, even if they are spending substantial amounts of time together with the baby, subsequent analysis has shown that the quality of their interactions are not very romantic, compassionate, interested, or affirming. This lack of positivity leads to more criticism and defensiveness in conflict, and couples are at the risk of falling into a more negative relationship spiral. Thus, couples who will face the change head on and recognize it as a distinct phase in their relationship will be better prepared.

CHAPTER 22

Managing Work-Life Balance

This study suggests pregnant women and their families often feel they are managing their workload by planning for their leave while pregnant, so when they actually return to work they do not feel their workload has shifted. However, once back at work, women reported leaving work early to pick up their child from childcare or missing events that were work-related due to childcare issues. The researchers suggest this lack of shift in workload responsibility "results in increased family stress, decreased work productivity, negative appraisals of family policies, and elevated rates of work-family and family-work conflicts, particularly among women." Like other research highlighted in this chapter, Gjerdingen, Center, and Froberg suggest this imbalance is preventable.

In this quantitative study, Gjerdingen, Center, and Froberg surveyed employed first-time mothers who were at least 4 months postpartum. They found mixed results: 15% of participants reported returning to work earlier than planned, 30% took more leave than planned, and the remaining 55% returned when planned. However, this study also indicated that women were more likely to return to work later than planned if that meant reducing or dropping childcare, while those under financial strain were more likely to return early. Gjerdingen et al. assigned a workaholic scale to 98 of the women who indicated they returned to work earlier than planned and noted a preference for returning to work earlier than planned when they had more workaholic tendencies. They cited other sources that found that over 60% of families with children under 5 years old state that they overwhelmingly face work conflicts in their requests for time off or flexibility. They also suggested that well-meaning workplace policies and practices may actually undermine working parents' work-life balance.

CHAPTER 23

CHAPTER 24

Seeking Support and Resources

I think a lot of couples encounter the challenge of shifting from being romantic partners or even cohabiting friends before they have kids. You spend so much time trying to figure out who you are as a couple and how to build this relationship together, so them when kids come you're no longer always friends or partners but also parents and at times you forget - I think it's the biggest challenge we've experienced. When you're stuck then you go back into couples therapy to reset again how your partners first and how much you love each other – be more than parents. At some point we accepted that we were more than parents, and then when we went back out into the real world we realized that just because you're more than parents your kids are all around you. When we had to find out who we were and what our goals were before we could define ourselves as parents, we went through that period of transition, then we had to deal with our relationships with our family and friends and acknowledge how relationships had changed.

In our last 2 years at the doctoral program, we've done workshops together about relationships and couples before, but we really didn't see ourselves as educators before. However, we were hunting for a local in-person class and we could not find one in our area. So we decided if we were looking for a class, maybe other people are and we tried launching a small pilot where we invited some friends and friends of friends to our place and we taught every single night for a week. Once we settled down to get married a few years later, we started brainstorming and that's how we started to collaborate as authors. We had so much to say about relationships, so we started to blog about relationships in Science of Relationships and Gay and Lesbian Relationships blogs. It gave so many reasons to collaborate and have conversations about how to present the science, so the movie When Strangers Click came to life after one of those conversations.

CHAPTER 25

Fostering Emotional Well-being

It's when you start nurturing emotional well-being in your relationship. Heather and Carl are intentionally finding several ways to foster it - within themselves and with each other. Heather spoke about cherishing her time pacing by herself. It gave her the space she needed to observe her feelings, think about them, name them, and then decide what to share. This is how the process worked for her: "If I can figure out what is going on inside my own head, heart, and body, I think I do a better job at explaining it out loud. I have been really trying to express where it's coming from, and that makes it a lot better." She also learned how incredibly important it is to listen to her body and its wisdom.

Fostering emotional well-being in yourself and each other is essential to staying strong in your couple relationship during this time of major life transition. For each of you, this involves taking good care of yourselves, but also staying connected and responsive to the support you need from each other. In this section, you will find clues on fostering emotional well-being in yourself and with your partner. Reflect on what you're already doing and explore new things that could enrich your support and self-care during this time of transition.

CHAPTER 26

Strengthening Your Connection

Given that much of the research on couples' relationships focuses on communication, I will start with communication. This is actually one of the simplest and most effective ways to maintain or improve your connection after having a baby. The problem is that it's way too easy to stop communicating, or to communicate poorly, about important aspects of life, couplehood, and parenthood, and the physical and psychological exhaustion you feel as a new parent makes you question how you find the time and energy for this communication. Despite the obstacles, remember to talk, or to listen, or to just "be" with your partner in the little time you have together before the baby wakes, after the baby falls asleep, or at another quiet moment. Turn to your partner first, after a long day of childcare or when you feel alone and overwhelmed. Avoid making the mistake of communicating only when something important arrives, such as a parenting disagreement or when you can't fight the sleep deprivation any longer; it makes your partner less open to connect.

Remember when your relationship only involved the two of you? The spontaneous getaways, leisurely mornings, and date nights? It's so common for life to become completely about the new baby and for a couple's entire identity to turn to parenthood. It's hard not to lose your couple identity—your rhythm, your unique routines, your inside jokes, and your way of being together—in the midst of work, childcare, chores, and sleep deprivation. Getting back your couple identity involves more than bringing balance or doing things together, but it's these little things that help, that can make the difference each day. Going back to your couple identity takes time and effort, but it's when you have this couple identity that you are stronger to face parenthood together.

CHAPTER 27

Celebrating Milestones

The birth celebration has similarities to both the traditional baby shower and to the more recent daddy's diaper party. In Kathleen Gallagher's research on nonresidential fathers, she reported observing young fathers and their new babies along with other men who celebrated the baby's birth. All the men simultaneously looked at the new baby dressed in new baby clothes. The room was silent as they watched the baby chubbily grasp and play with her tiny, innocent toes, oblivious to the captivated audience. Then, glowing, each man took his turn at what he wanted to do. Finally, Baby Daddy brought out his video camera. He commented that all babies do the same thing but that he really needed to film his baby. With her baby next to her, BABY MAMA whispered, "They all really need to film their baby. All over the world, when a man has a baby, they all really need to just film their baby."

By inviting Dad to give physical care to the new baby, he should be the one to give physical care. For example, get up at night or give comfort when the child is in pain. This is physically incompatible with his fatherhood role. In addition to unusual gender patterns in the baby's physical care, bolstered by the gentle support of his partner, there is a presence of fathers with the baby and both parents' recognition of how much mothers achieved while pregnant and achieved at birth - along with many other moments. Babies are born all the time, but to a father, they are all unique and valuable, extraordinary objects. There is only one baby in the entire world who is his child. The desire to celebrate, and even honor, the birth of their baby seems innate. Of all the observances fathers seek, it seems that the most popular for Baby Daddy - especially for young fathers or those in high school or college - is a birth celebration.

CHAPTER 28

Reflecting on Parenthood

This next consideration should not be overlooked because it is important to address and move forward with a stated goal and some concrete steps, even while being flexible. Children are a great grounding presence in people's lives and can provide a focus that helps you as a couple to grow, but it is important to be aware of what your goals are and to be sure you're doing what you can to move in the right direction. Setting goals is important to make certain that you aren't feeling stagnant in your relationship and you aren't finding too much stress, souring your feelings of commitment. With the right preparation and planning, you can enter parenthood feeling prepared and ready to create the best life possible for your little one.

When you are thinking about entering parenthood, you need to think about how you want to approach it as a couple. It is very important to embrace the idea of mutually contributing to the child-rearing experience, to determine what "fair" means to you and your partner, as well as think about what you will do as a couple to maintain and grow your relationship. Some important questions to consider are: "What do you want your family to look like? How does your childhood influence how you want to raise your own children?

How will you maintain or grow your relationship?" First, you will need to address the type of roles you each want to take. Do you both want to work outside the home? Do you want one partner to stay at home, or only work part-time? Who will be the primary caretaker during the workday, or during the night when the baby may need to be fed, put back to sleep, or just want their mommy? This is a very big discussion and one that is really important to have. How will things change should either of you be promoted or laid off? Discussing this upfront and being able to come to an agreement, even if it means continuous discussions as you move forward, is very important.

CHAPTER 29

Embracing Parenthood as a Journey

Becoming a parent is a monumental event, for everyone involved really, from beyond the walls of our immediate tiny family, all the way from our ancestors' past, to the future lives of our children. And it's quite the expedition we find ourselves undertaking; because no matter how many parents you've been, or plan to be, you are never prepared for the reality of parenthood until you are in it. That's when you find not only those oh-so-unexpected experiences, some too beautiful for words, some too hard to bear; but also, dare I say, it is the time you become 100% invested in being a parent.

I've found that the best way to approach (well, many aspects of life) is to take it on as a journey: with a bit of adventure, some mystery, and a lot of exploration thrown in for good measure. And let's not forget the ups, the downs, the highs and the lows! Well, here's another on the list for us to venture through: parenthood. Here, there's guaranteed "adventure" and "mystery", yes, without a doubt in my mind. What perhaps makes parenthood more unique for me is the nature of the "exploration": in this journey, our girls and the two of us and our relationship with each other, all grow. There are lessons to be learned, wisdom to be sought after, and knowledge to be gained. These three rewards, hidden away in the corners of the world, reveal themselves in gold only to those few brave wanderers who dare to explore that uncharted territory.

CHAPTER 30

Embracing Parenthood
as a Team

In a study of social support and determinants of marital adjustment in early parenthood, mothers who endorsed higher spousal support from pregnancy to the postpartum period reported less negative marital change over time. In other words, spousal support from partners seemed to be more important in the early postpartum period in terms of marital quality. This finding is corroborated in research on how couples communicate in pregnancy and in the first 6 weeks after their baby's birth. Emotional support provided to their partners was found to enhance couple adaptation to the new parental role. Couples who reported high rates of partner support during the transition to their roles as parents were shown to adapt positively to their new roles by openly communicating, relying on shared humor and affection for each other, in addition to using problem-solving skills. There was a similar finding that showed that low levels of support from the mother's partner were a strong predictor of later postpartum depressive symptoms and marital dissatisfaction. These findings combined imply that the level of support provided by a partner to their loved one during the antenatal period and through the transition into parenthood may shape the relationship dynamics that emerge, which could cause stress and impact family equilibrium both positively and negatively.

The transition to parenthood is a significant milestone for couples and may influence the overall health and well-being of the family. The Postpartum Transition for Partner Empowerment (PTPE) intervention aims to help couples transition smoothly into their new parental roles by focusing on spousal empowerment, co-parenting, and shared responsibility. Several modules in the PTPE intervention focus on values and principles that can be introduced to help couples transition into parenthood with less stress and improve overall family function in their new roles as parents. These principles are founded in relationship theory. Relationship satisfaction during the transition to parenthood (TTP) can be impacted by several factors, including sleep deprivation, changes in financial status, and difficulty in resolving conflict. Also, pregnancy, childbirth, and attending to the newborn can have a negative effect on a woman's health, which in turn can intensify levels of stress and impact relationship dynamics. Strategies that have been proposed include improving communication and mutual support, teaching couples relaxation and coping mechanisms to help deal with stress, identifying existing and new sources of social support, and enhancing coming to a consensus on goals and expectations for parenting.

CHAPTER 31

Conclusion

It is important to note that the transition to parenthood is not a purely technical challenge, but one that exposes couples to profound questions that resonate. Only by being aware of these concerns and frequently revisiting the self-understanding of their own family, however it may be defined, can couples become aware of the 'hidden curriculum' underlying couple relationships. They can become familiar with the most essential experiences and challenges and recognize the phases that they will go through. Consequently, becoming a parent together also becomes an opportunity for the couple's self-understanding and for the development of a sustainable partnership.

Transitioning to parenthood brings new experiences and challenges, as well as joys. For many individuals, becoming a parent is an important identity shift. Similarly, becoming a parent simultaneously shifts romantic partners' interactions regarding division of family labor, emotional burdens, and the relational processes that brought them together. This involves a cascade of events as these individuals assimilate new roles together as partners and parents. But how these processes play out can vary widely due to diverse experiences in families, communities, and cultural contexts. Although diverse pathways may privilege different groups of people, it may have similar positive and negative consequences for individuals' well-being. Knowing this, how do we provide equality for all people who seek to be not only "partners" but the best parents, and ultimately the best role models for their children?